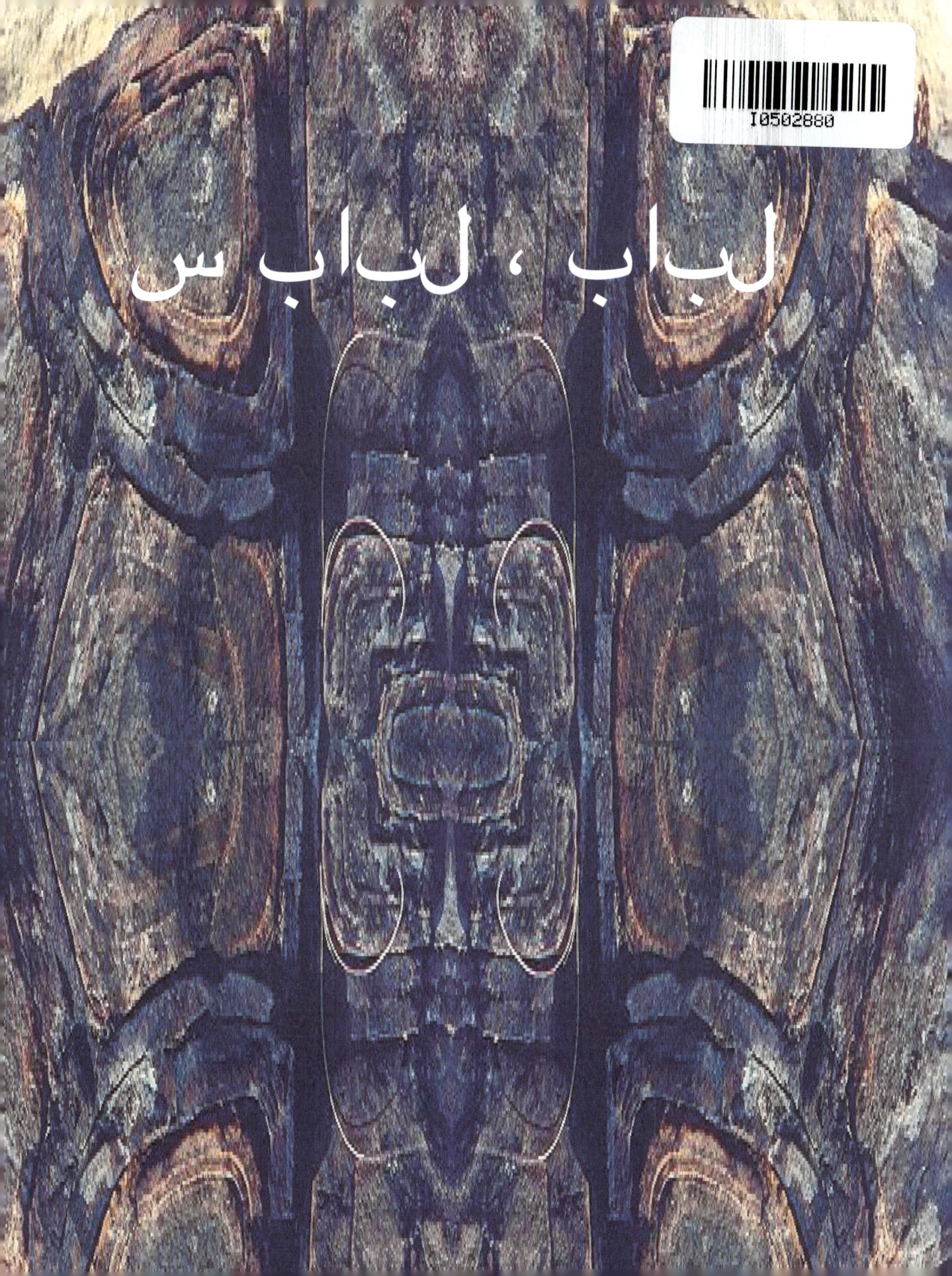

لباب ، لباب س

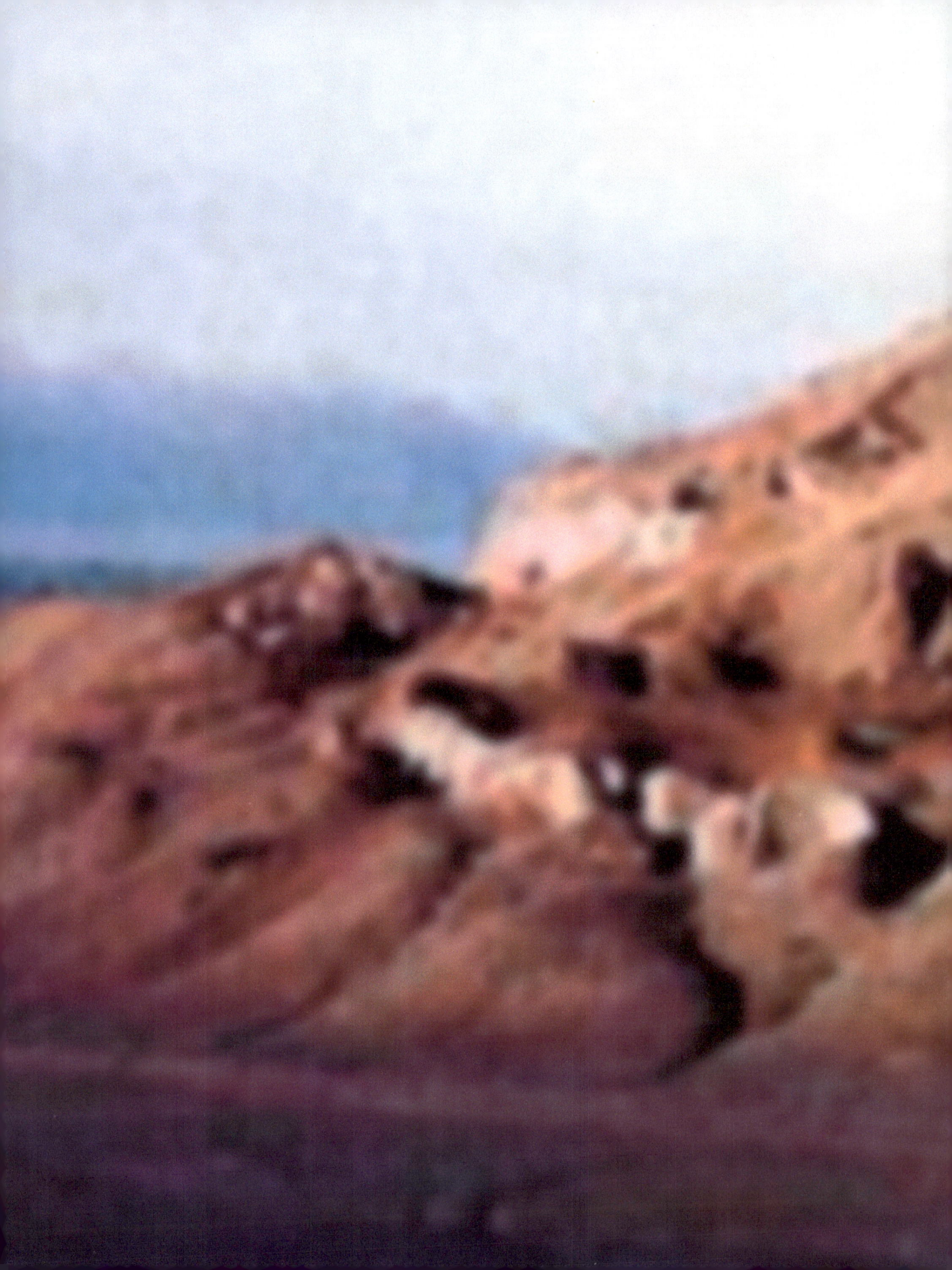

babylon

ministry of misinformation

a cinephrastic surveillance
counter-invented

by mIEKAL aND

xerox sutra editions
west lima, wisconsin

You have been invited to interact with
Babylon Ministry of Misinformation online at:
http://www.spidertangle.net/babili/index.html

ISBN 1-440401-56-X
EAN-13 978-1-44040156-5

published by

Xerox Sutra Editions
10375 County Hway Alphabet
La Farge, WI 54639

perspicacity@xexoxial.org

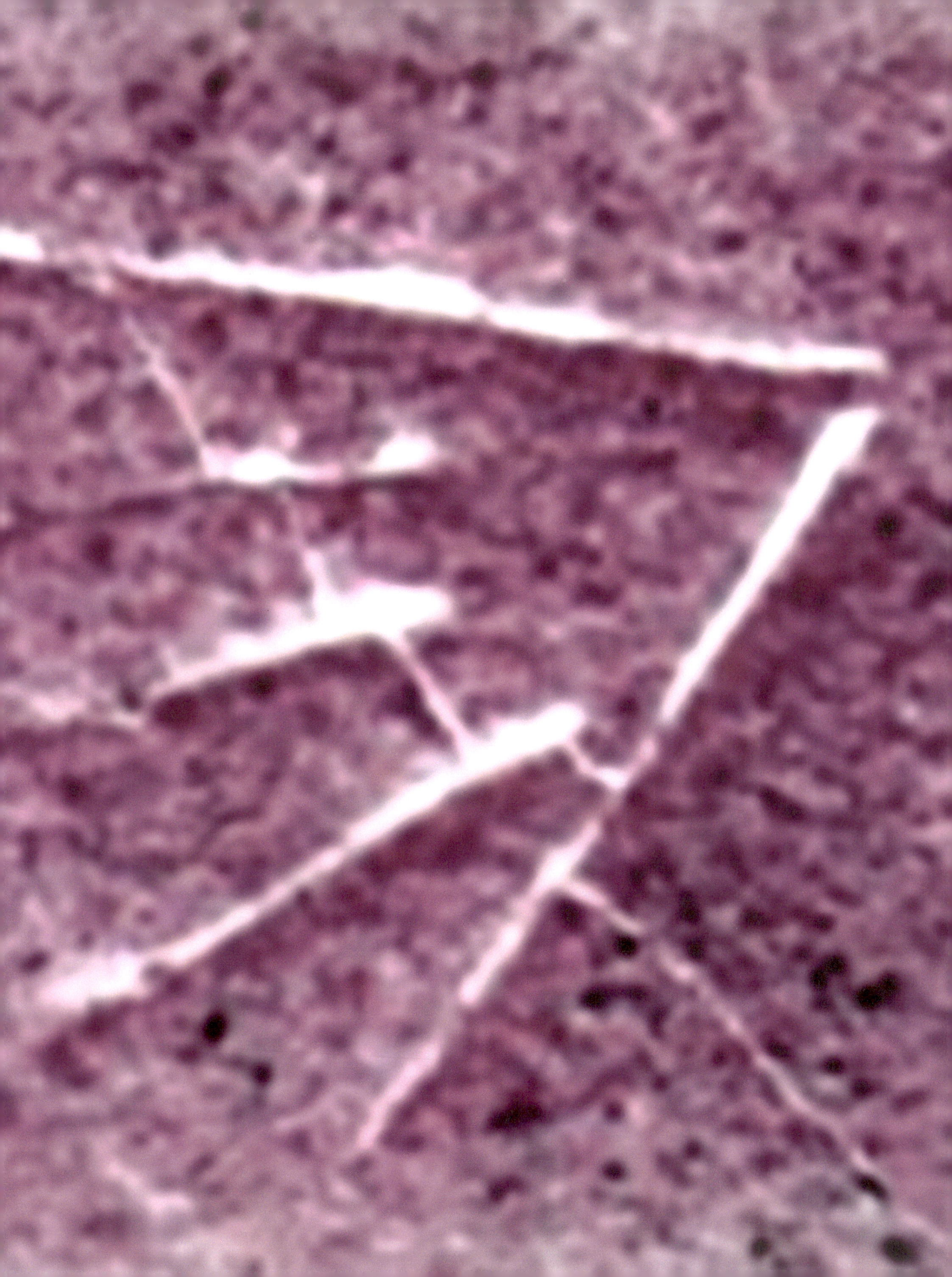

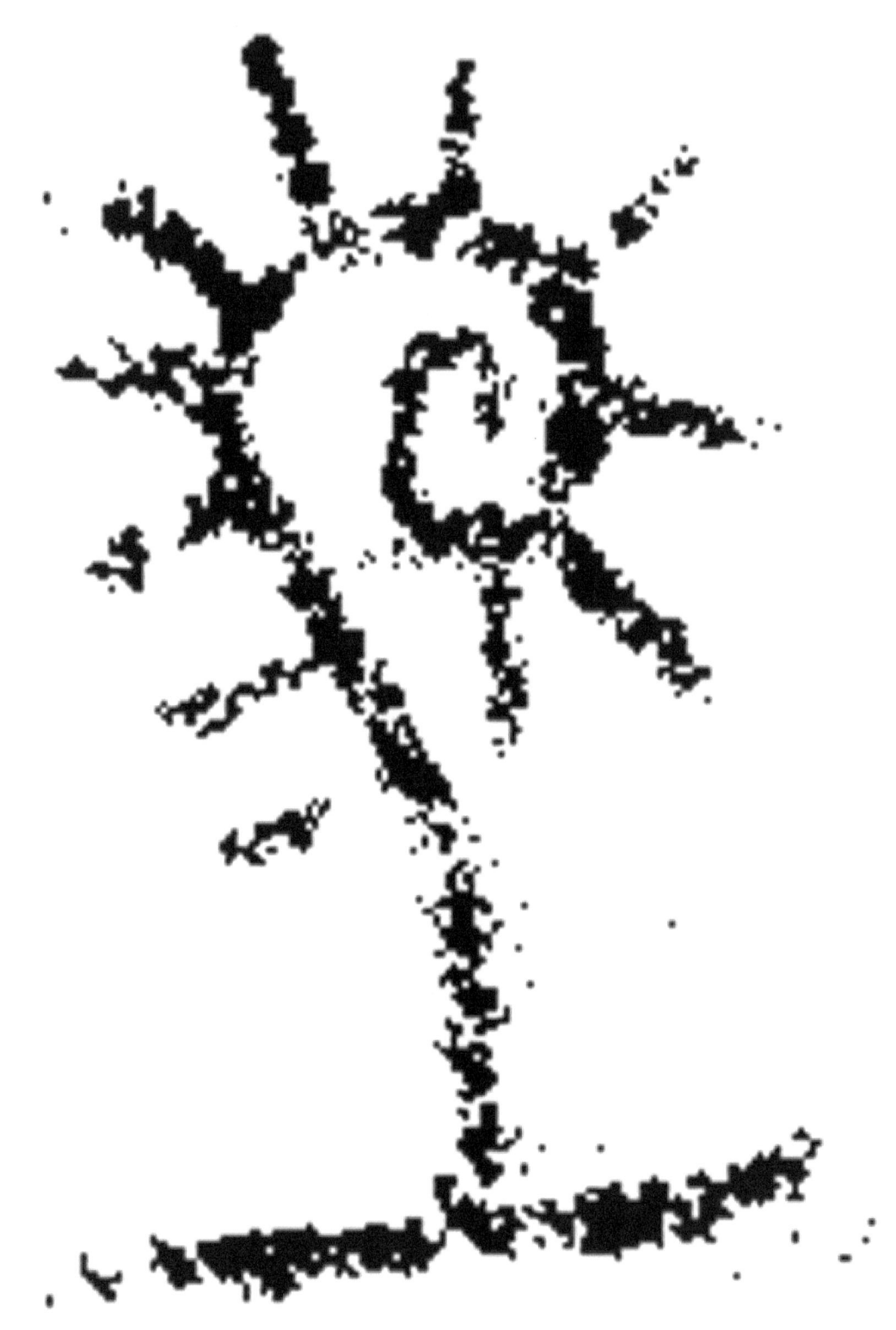

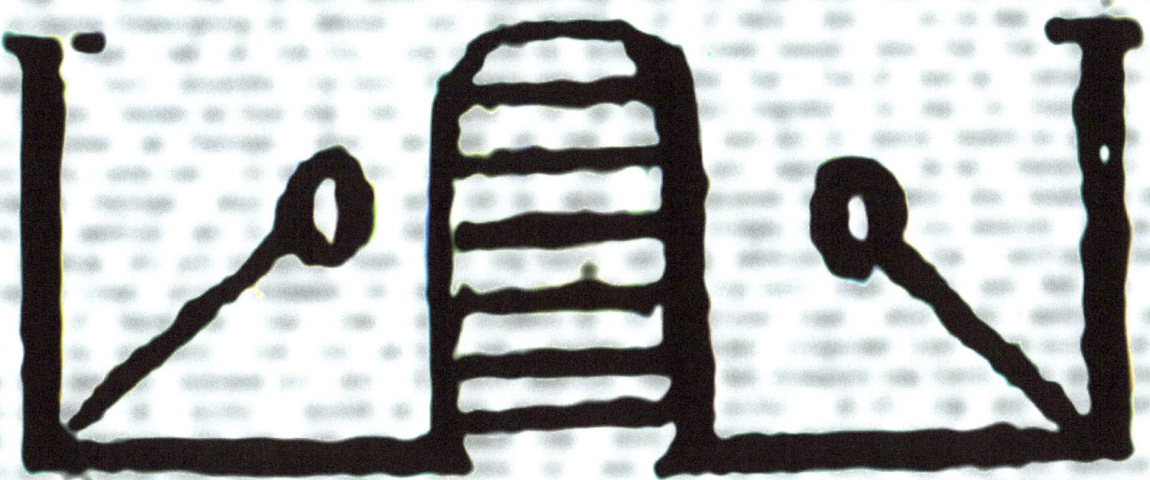

"impersonate peaceful truths, reconsider violent non-objectivity"

CognateOfUr

It has been brought to the attention of the proto-civilians of the region of the Tigris-Euphrates that at the event of the 21st Century AD much of our culture's 5000 plus years of future invention & evolution of civilization will be lost, forgotten, erased, appropriated, burned, americanized, exploited, & trampled on. In 3000 BCE The BABYLON MINISTRY OF MISINFORMATION had the vision to initiate a node to witness & remember the fragments of glyphs, signs, letterforms, ledgers, tablets, proclamations, lyrics & texts which repeated Expansionist-Nations will seek to overthrow. We are seeking the inventive actions of all artists & poets of the future to help remember WhatCouldBe.

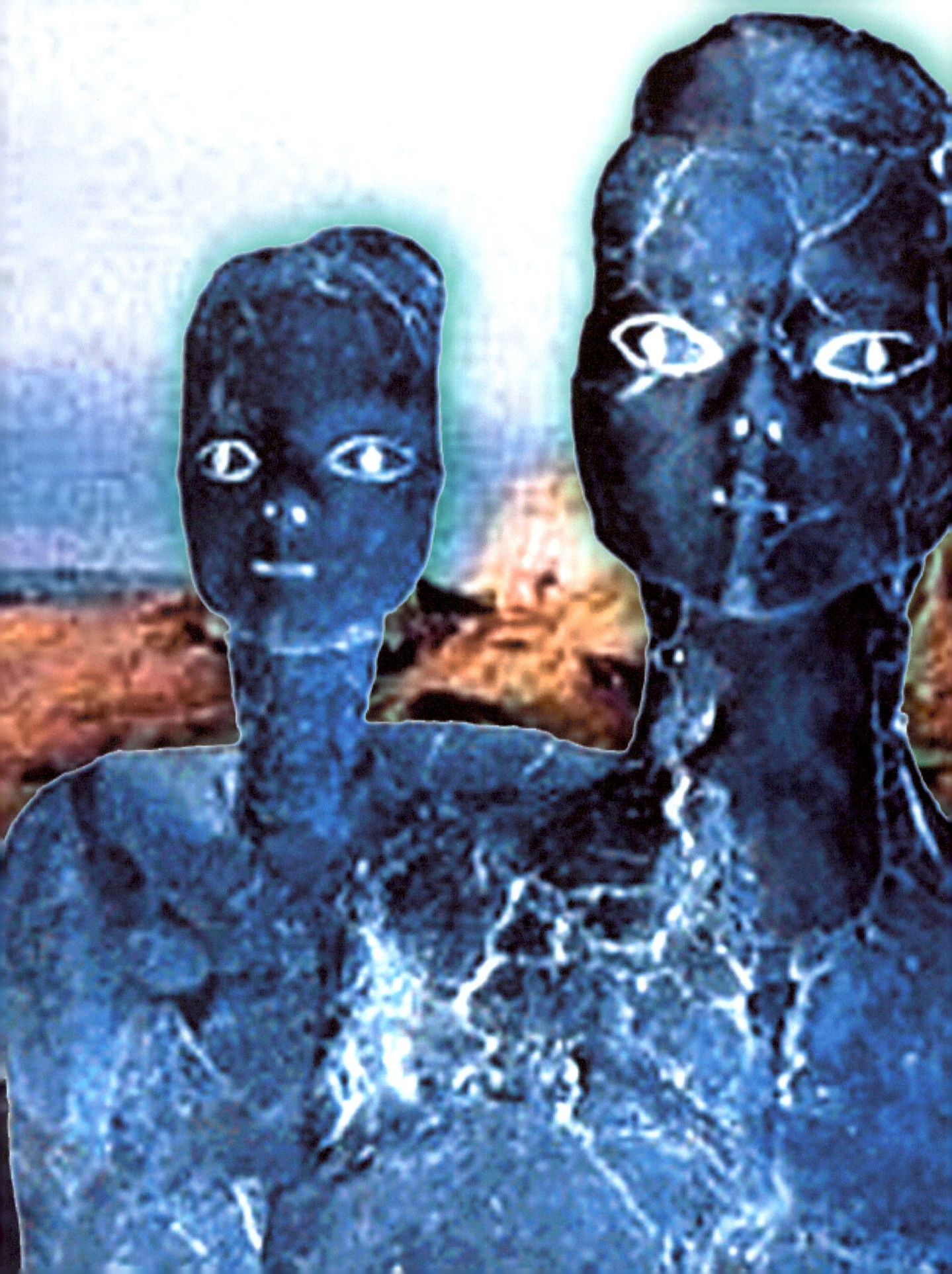

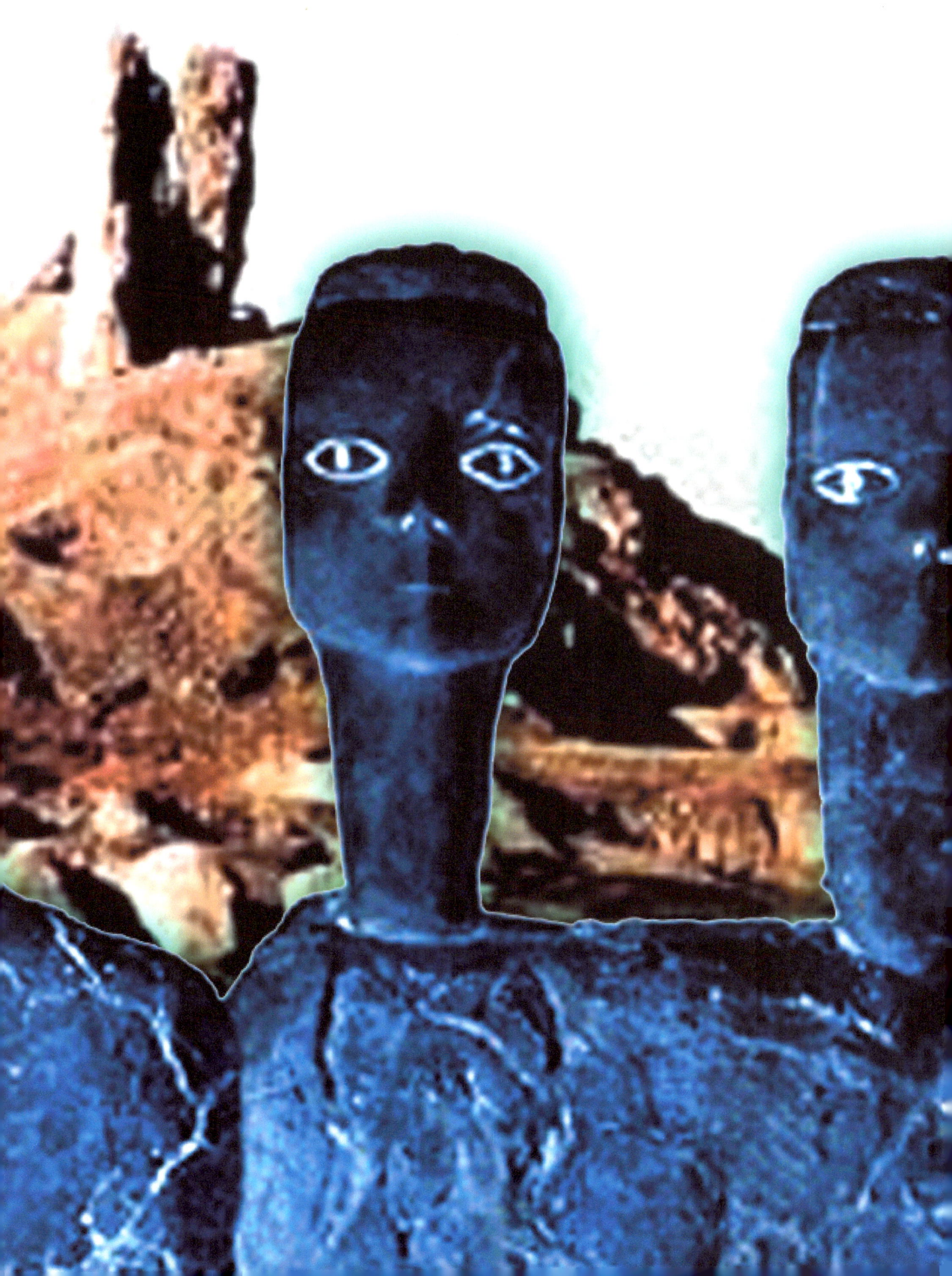

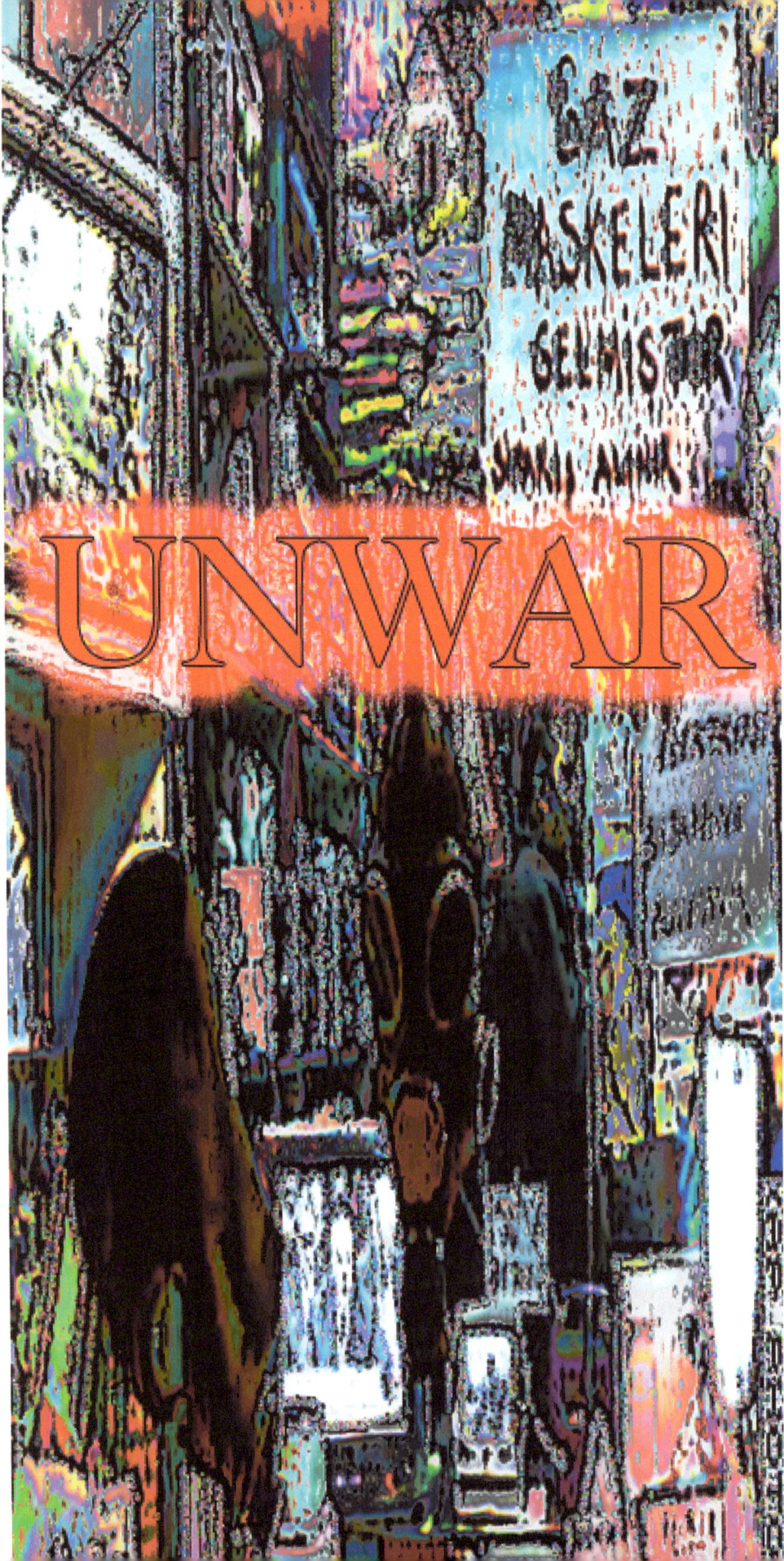

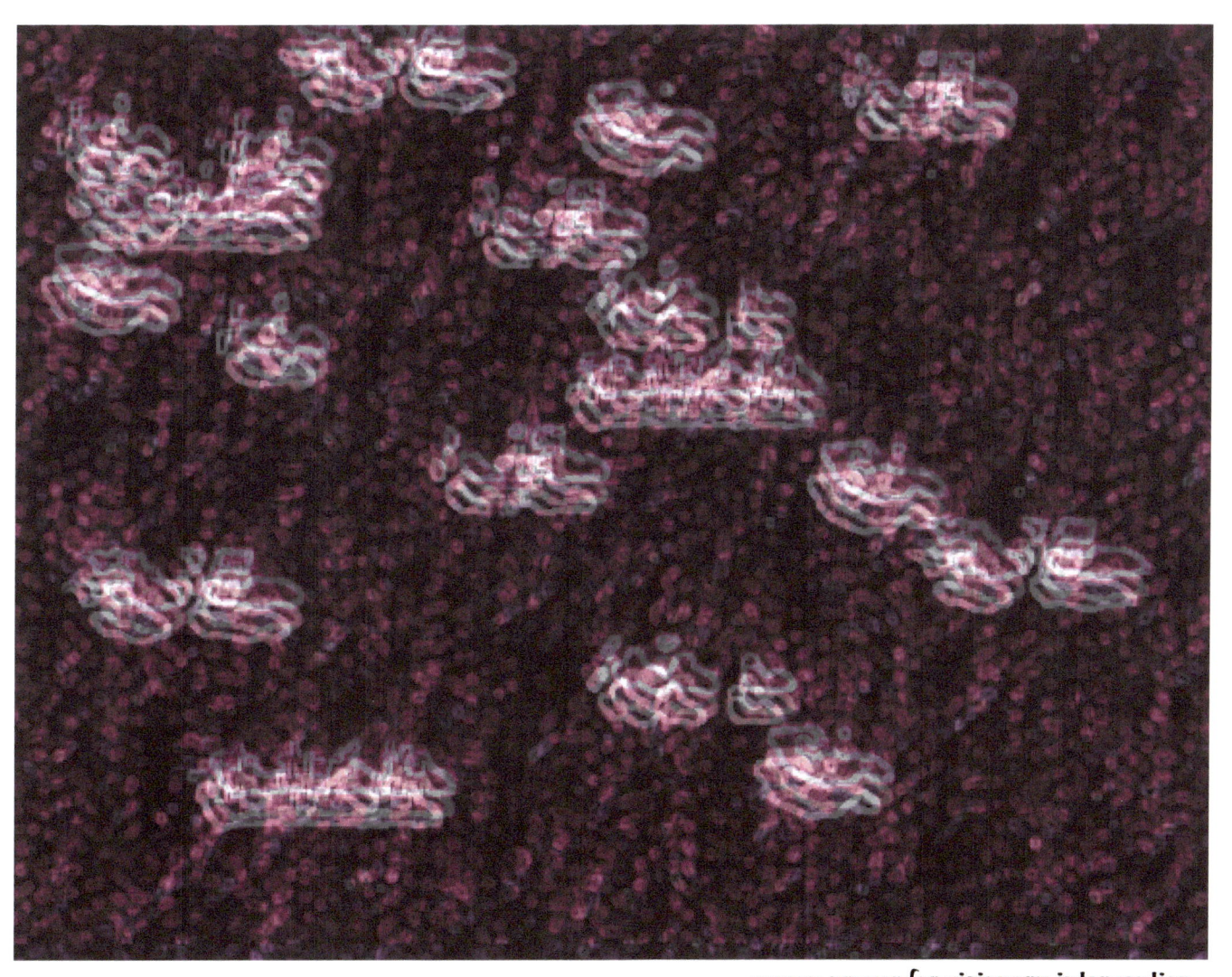

cuman prayer for visionary intervention

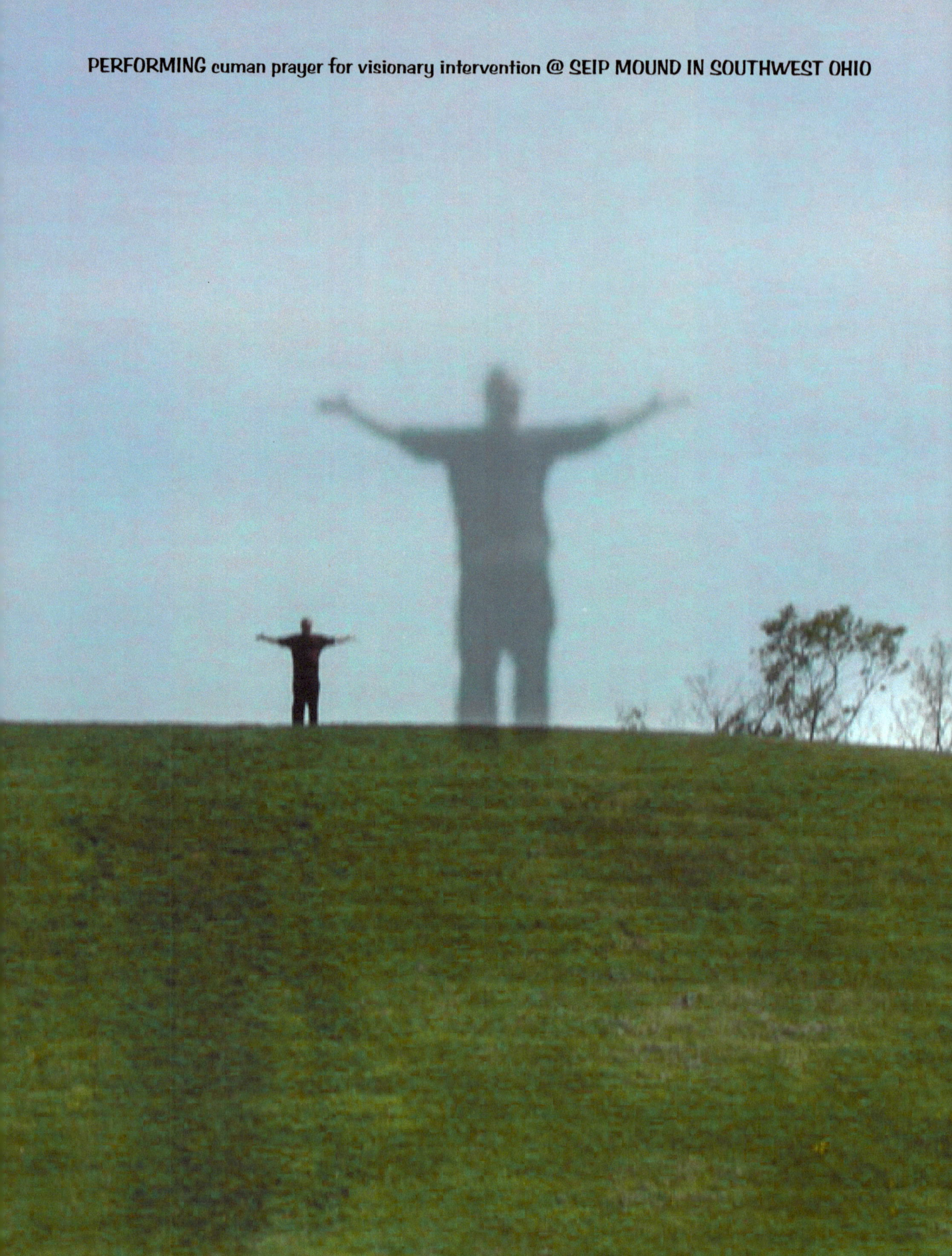

PERFORMING cuman prayer for visionary intervention @ SEIP MOUND IN SOUTHWEST OHIO

Seems to be
lament
on command
how she
under
sense of
doom
for that
storm
upon
tears
heavy with
trembling
before that days
days within
no happy
days
that night of cruel
I could not flee
destruction
sudden
at night
dreams
of a sudden
oblivion upon
this bitter
my land
had I come

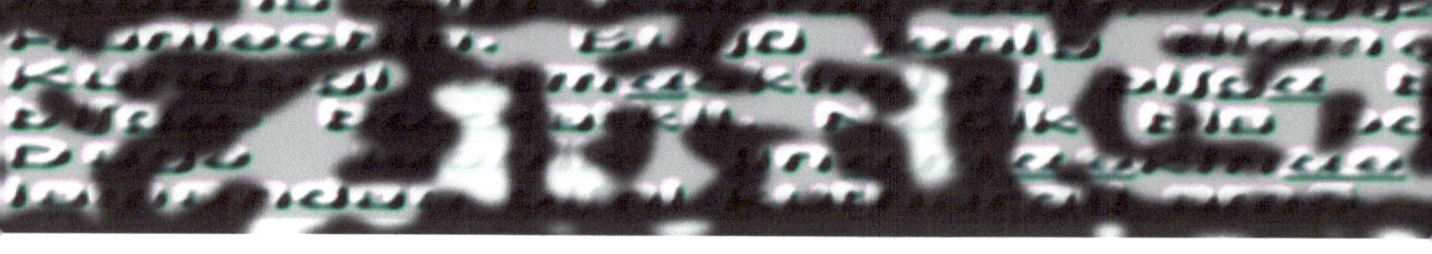

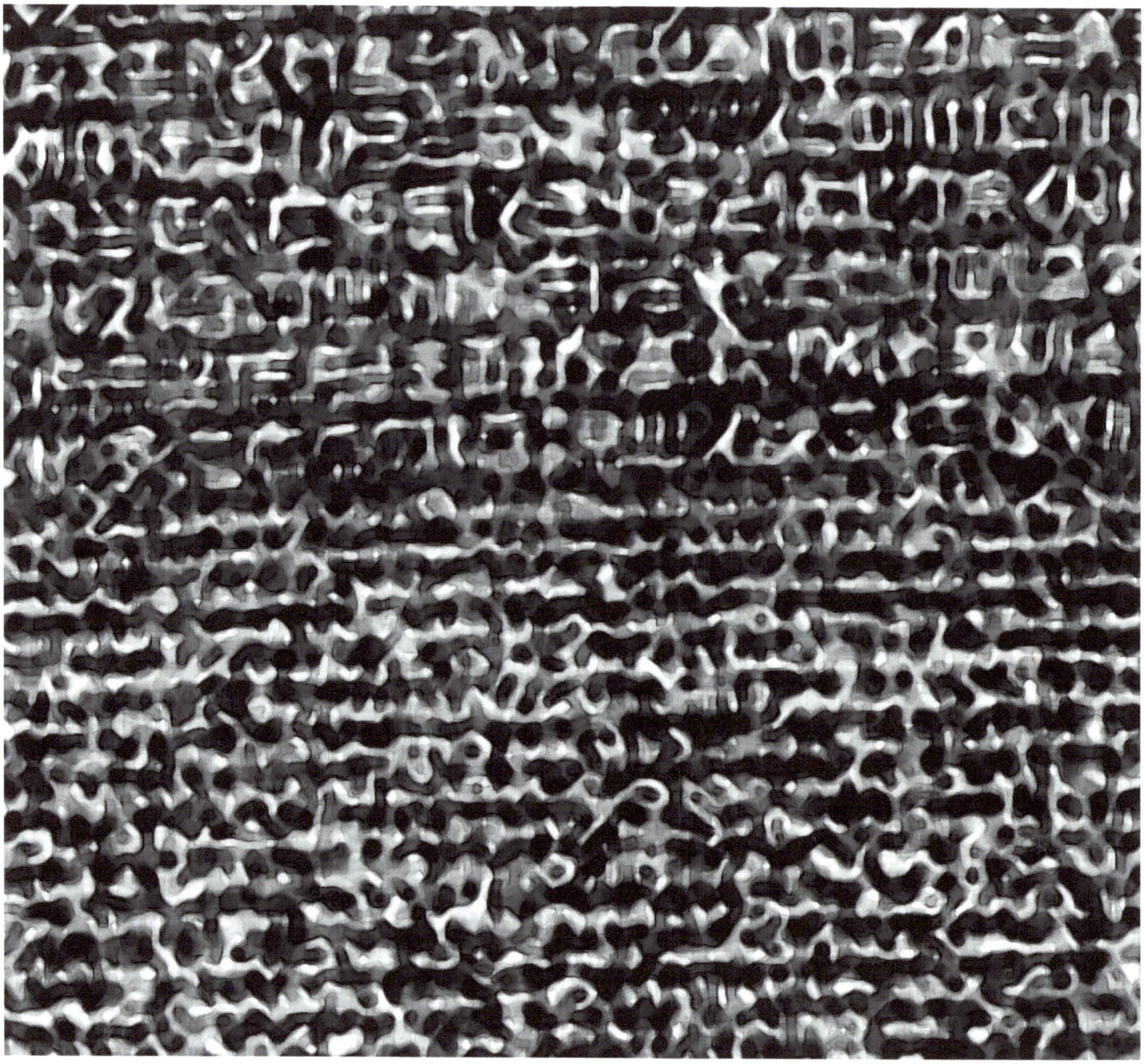

DESTINY GLITCH (reconstructed scrollwork)

Yet to be discovered in an architectural dig of the Arboretum of Non-Intervention
Preponderance

slipshod translation of industrial_fragment.jpg
"THOU SHALT NOT DESECRATE THE BIRTHPLACE OF LANGUAGE IN THE NAME OF IMPERIALIST SCHIZOPHRENY"

winds the desert flaming scorched ordered by hate wears away the country veiled it that day was a ruin left a ruin on that day the people not potshards littered the walls in wide streets, where feasting crowds jumbled in all bodies in open with dancers blood like metal dissolved the sun the moon appeals to what my city turned away from

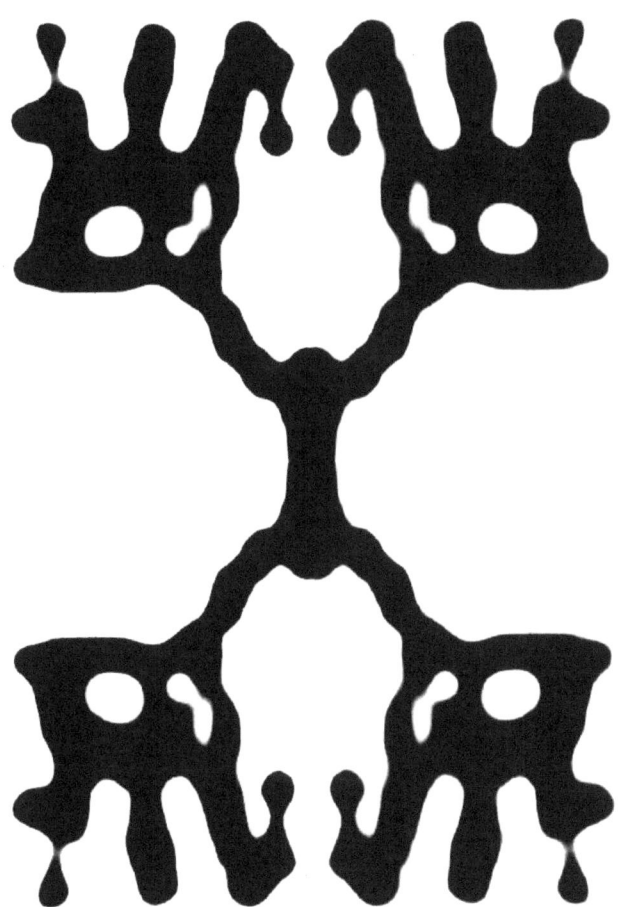

opportunity_sigil.gif

he created created place

he constructed

he built

he established

the mother I know not

my city is situation on

the Euphrates

my secret brought me

in my entrance

the river did overflow me

carried me

irrigator irrigator of heart lifted

irrigator own son

irrigator his gardener

was a gardener

and for peoples

mountain destroyed mountains

a-na za-mi-bi-im. kalag-ga-na cir-bi-im.

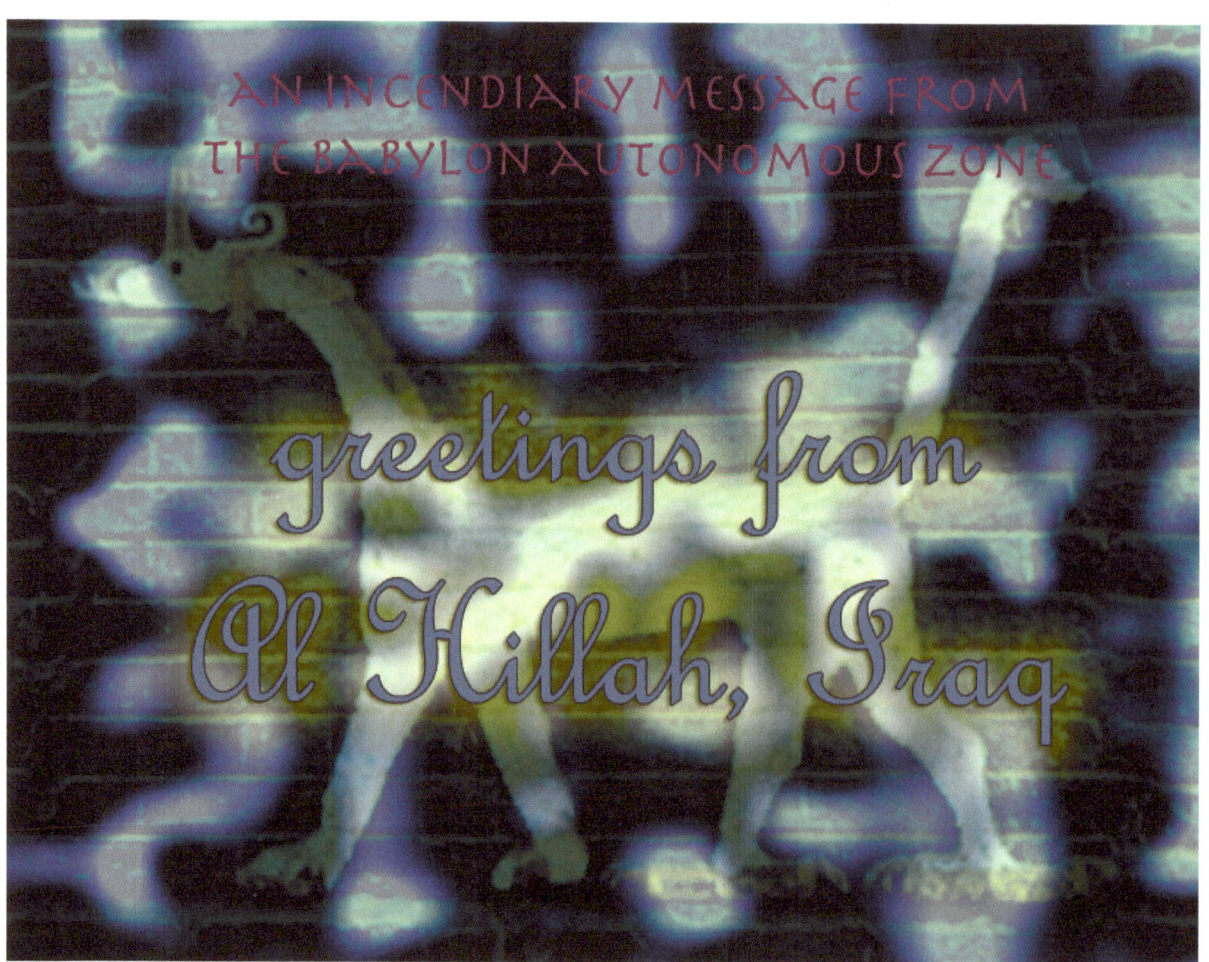

AN INCENDIARY MESSAGE FROM
THE BABYLON AUTONOMOUS ZONE

greetings from
Al Hillah, Iraq

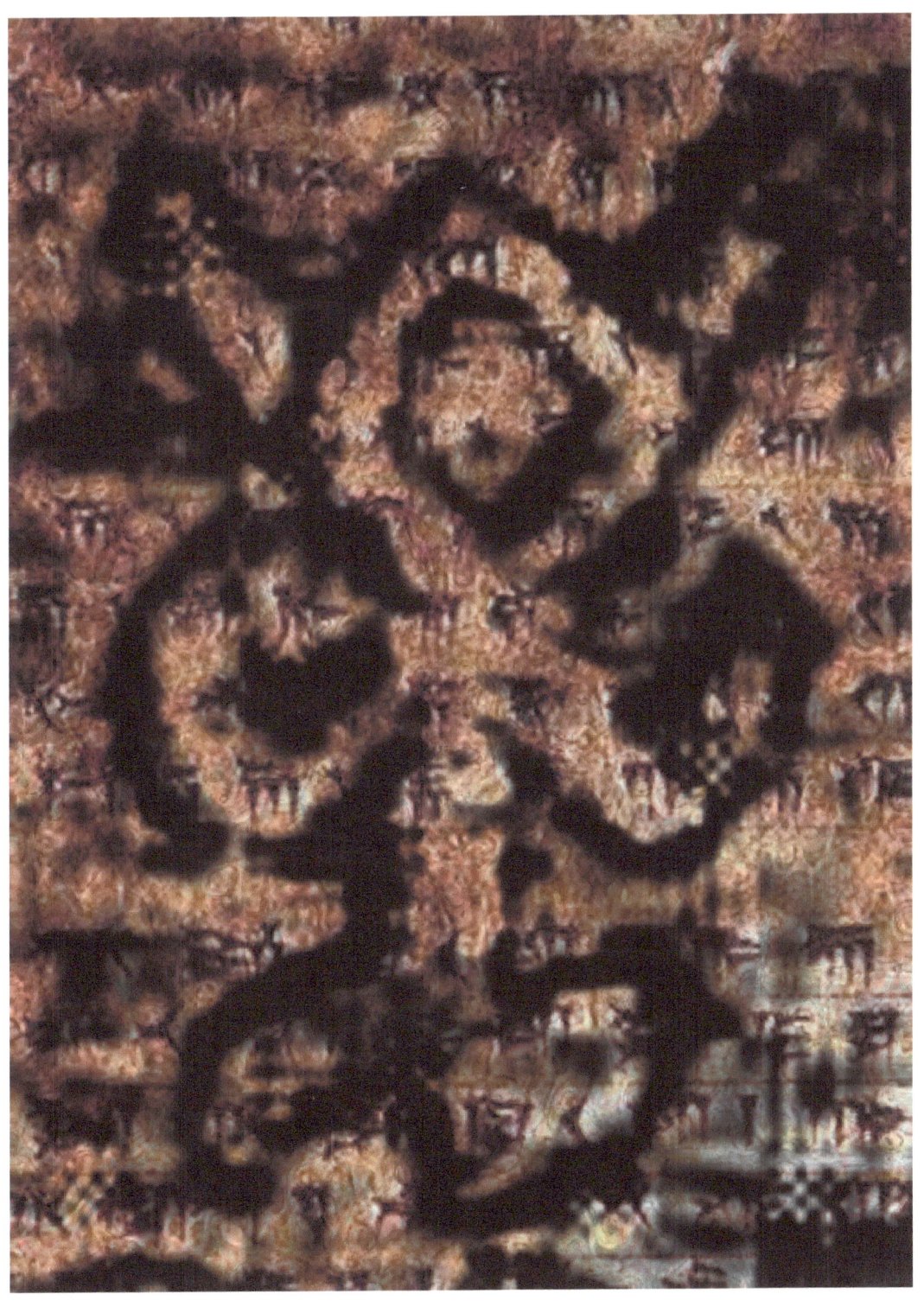

March 20, 2003 ~ A L I E N S   H A V E   L A N D E D   I N   B A B Y L O N

Sitting in their holy place
tremble, stricken
their flesh prickles all over
a red-hot terror
paralyzes our whole country
My lord, that which has been created (here) no one has
created (before).

Without you no destiny at all is determined, no clever
counsel is granted favor.
To run, to escape, to quiet and to pacify are yours,
Inanna.

listen!
I the Lady
came near
and the mountain did not fear

Enheduanna 2300 BCE Sumer

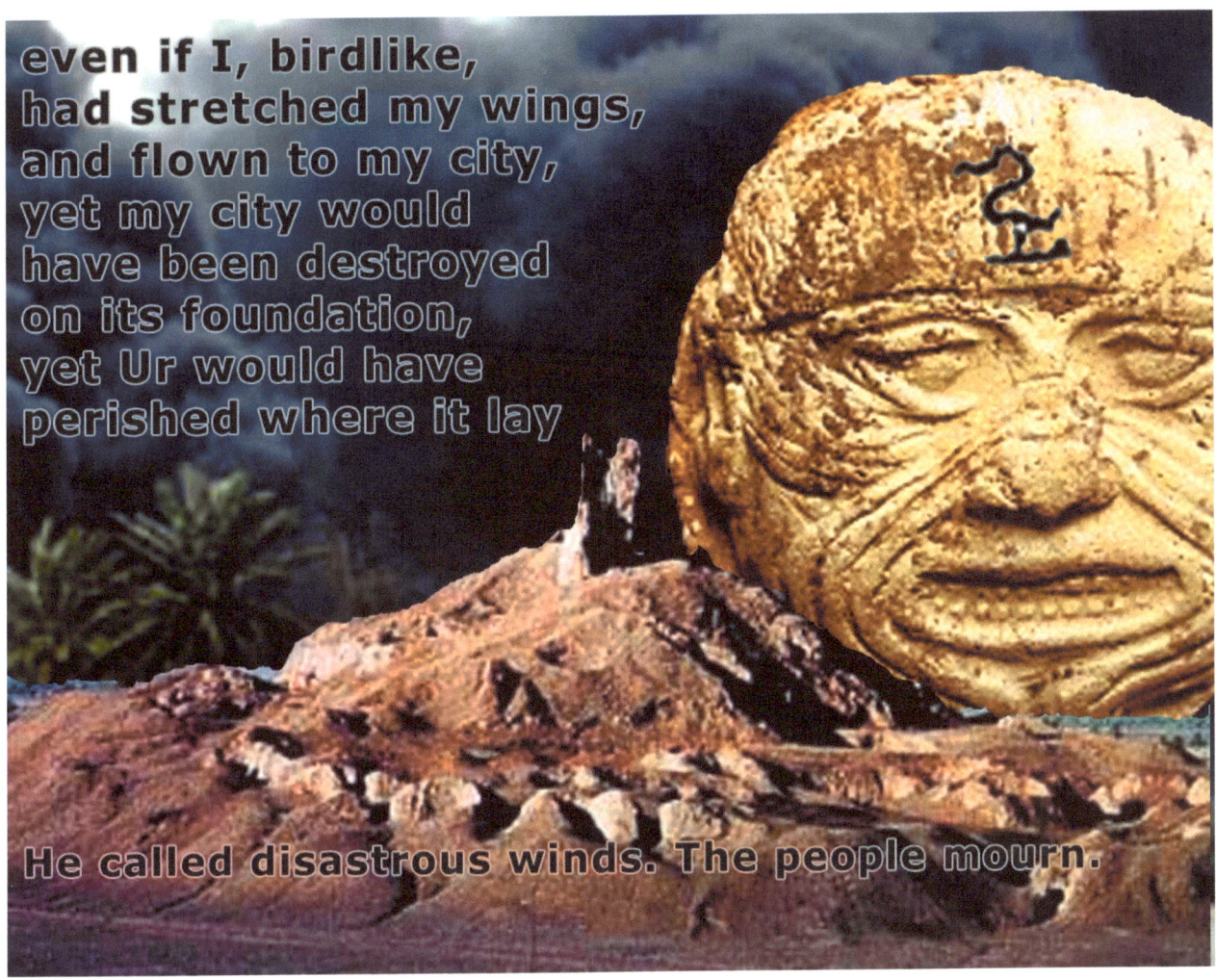

even if I, birdlike,
had stretched my wings,
and flown to my city,
yet my city would
have been destroyed
on its foundation,
yet Ur would have
perished where it lay

He called disastrous winds. The people mourn.

Jongling, binging, and rottling accampanied hoathen calts, and the frunzying shiwms of a duzen acstatic croes intaxicated the messes. Omid this iuphoric ferewell fuast of a deing covilization.

Crucial foreclosure on the Battologeo of not our Place.

to have been changed
a lasting
not granted from
the country first settled
who ever
has been uprooted

do not worry
a house of
place not made
no tree
no brick
no house
no thrones established
not been built

the deep formed
the holy
the dwelling lands
in the midst of water
those days

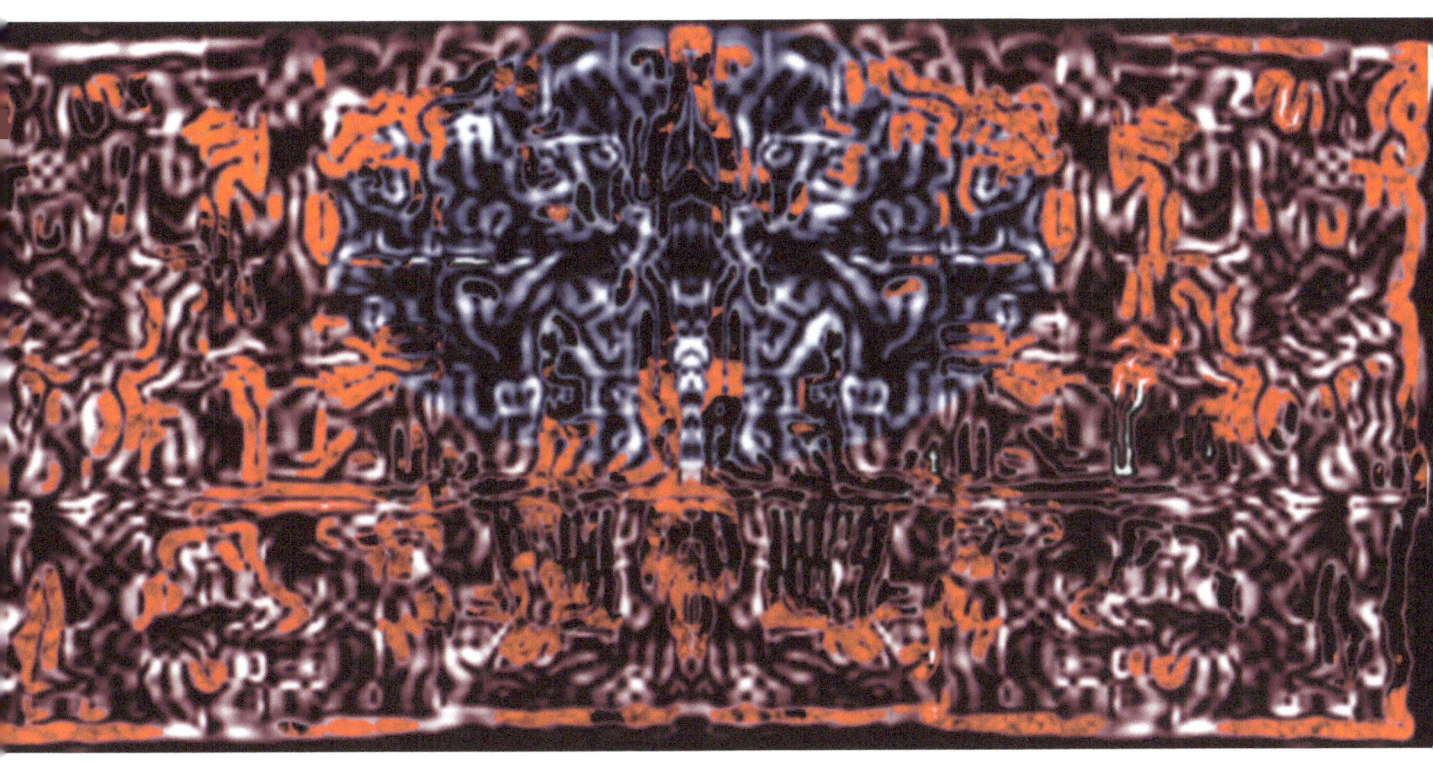

Spectral deconstruction of a fragment from the Tartarian Tablets, 5000 BC Tartaria Romania

do you not worry! Leave your city!

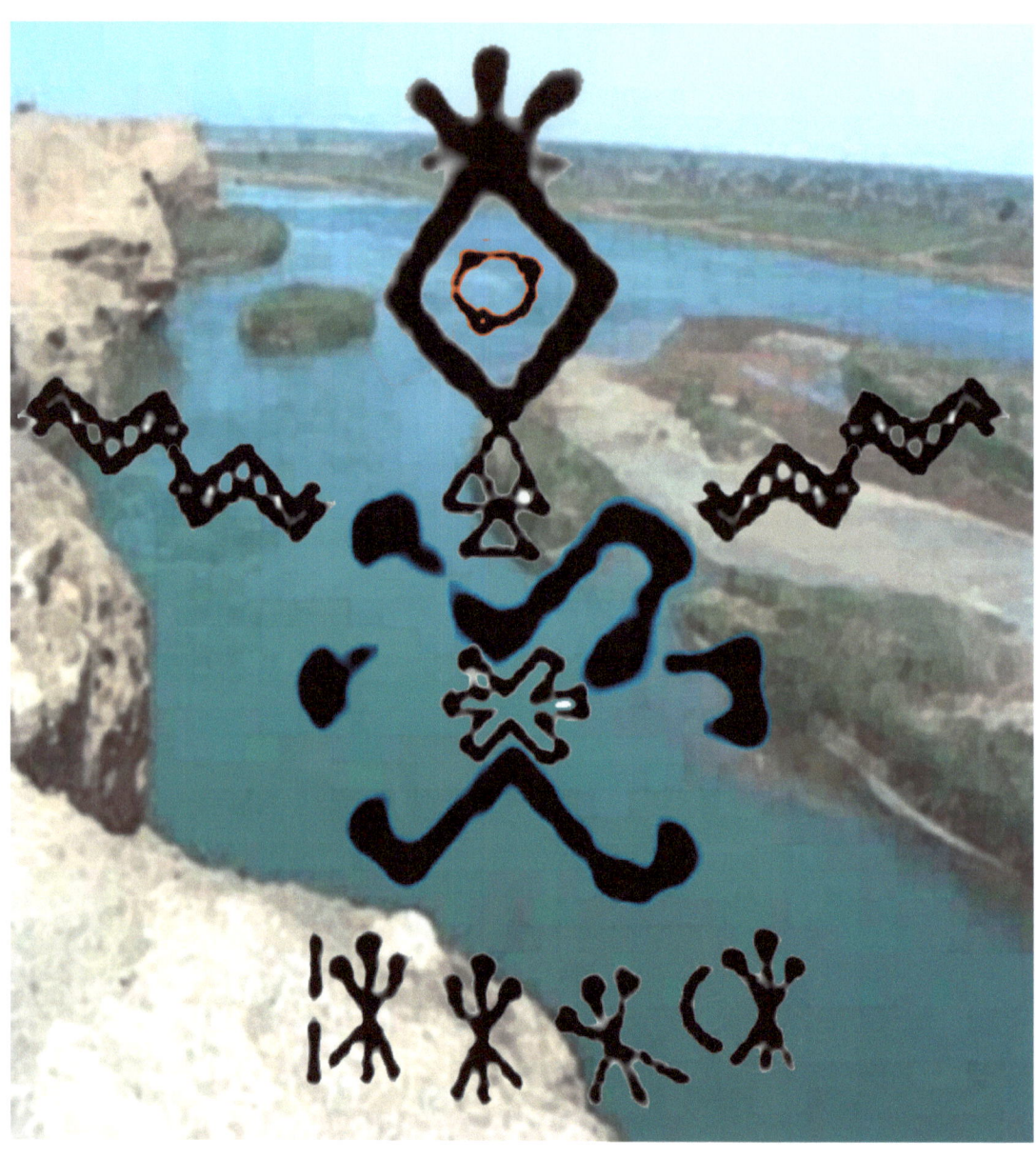

Who will water the HANGING GARDENS?

why have fruits no longer fruits
no longer bread and
fold again into my city
its loneliness again into your arms

into your arms let emerge Ur
people expand the ways
restored you
the heart wasted weeping flutes
grow weeping
spend the day concerned
there is a decree
a command not known

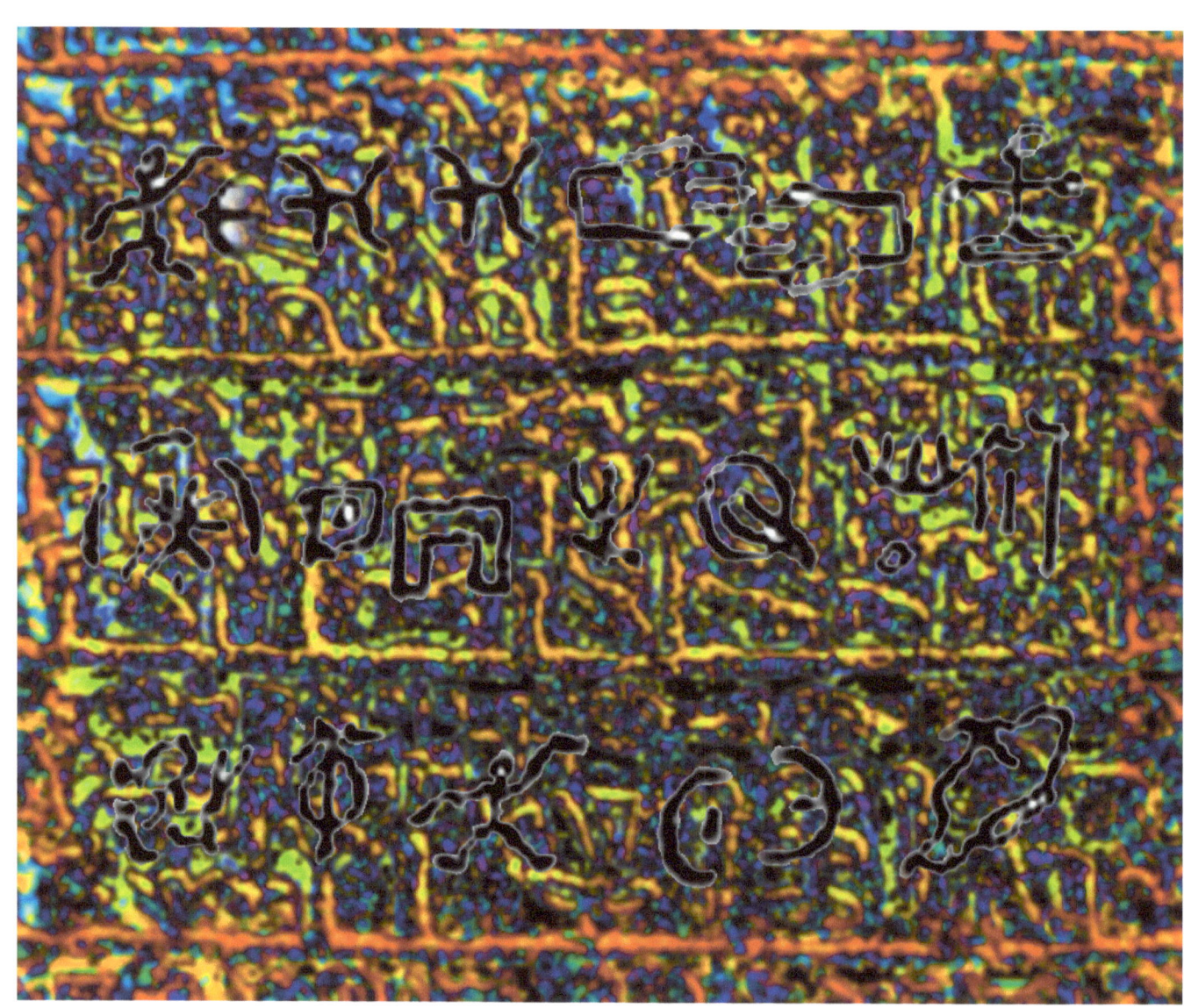

3rd Millennium BCE decrypted JPG of the Artfully Built Mountain (some doubt about dating of
pictograms)

Book of Saphah: "Zarathustra worked no miracles. He said miracles were the tricks of spirits and mortals. The highest of all good was to do good, and be good." [left to right, top to bottom]

1. You will Live in the Moment. Fleeing your Homeland is your only Option. Birds of Terror follows You where you Go.

2. Bodies are Lying Everywhere.

3. Burn Shadow of Bodies Lying Everywhere.

4. Shaking Inverse Hands is Keystroke of the Invasion of Peace.

5. Body in Balance. Walk in Other's Shoes.

6. Chaos Dancing Planetary Jiggle.

7. The Beast of Civilization is Weighted Down by Neaderthal Conqueror Consciousness.

8. Only some Remain Free.

9. Earth is a Comet of Comic Devolution. Entrophy Exhausts the Core.

10. The Seed of Reaching-Skyward Shelters those who Know.

11. Coagulants of Many Nations Catalyze.

12. Omega Triangulated. Maximum Diversity Achieved.

13. Expanding Forces of what a Body is & what a Body can Be.

14. One Ear listening to other Ear in Perpetuity.

15. Planet Spaceship is Seed of Next Lifeform.

"I am the lekythos of Tateie; may whoever steals me be blind."

We knocked on the door and were invited in by a 92 year old resident of the area. The hill folk of Oklahoma are a warm, hospitable people but the old gentleman could not recall hearing of any tablets, though he did know much of what had occurred locally for most of the 20th century. He told us of numerous places where rare flints were to be found and mentioned an "old furnace" that a big timber company had pushed down with bulldozers.

Phoenician script of 8th Century BCE Byblos.
Paraphonetic thermal transcription.

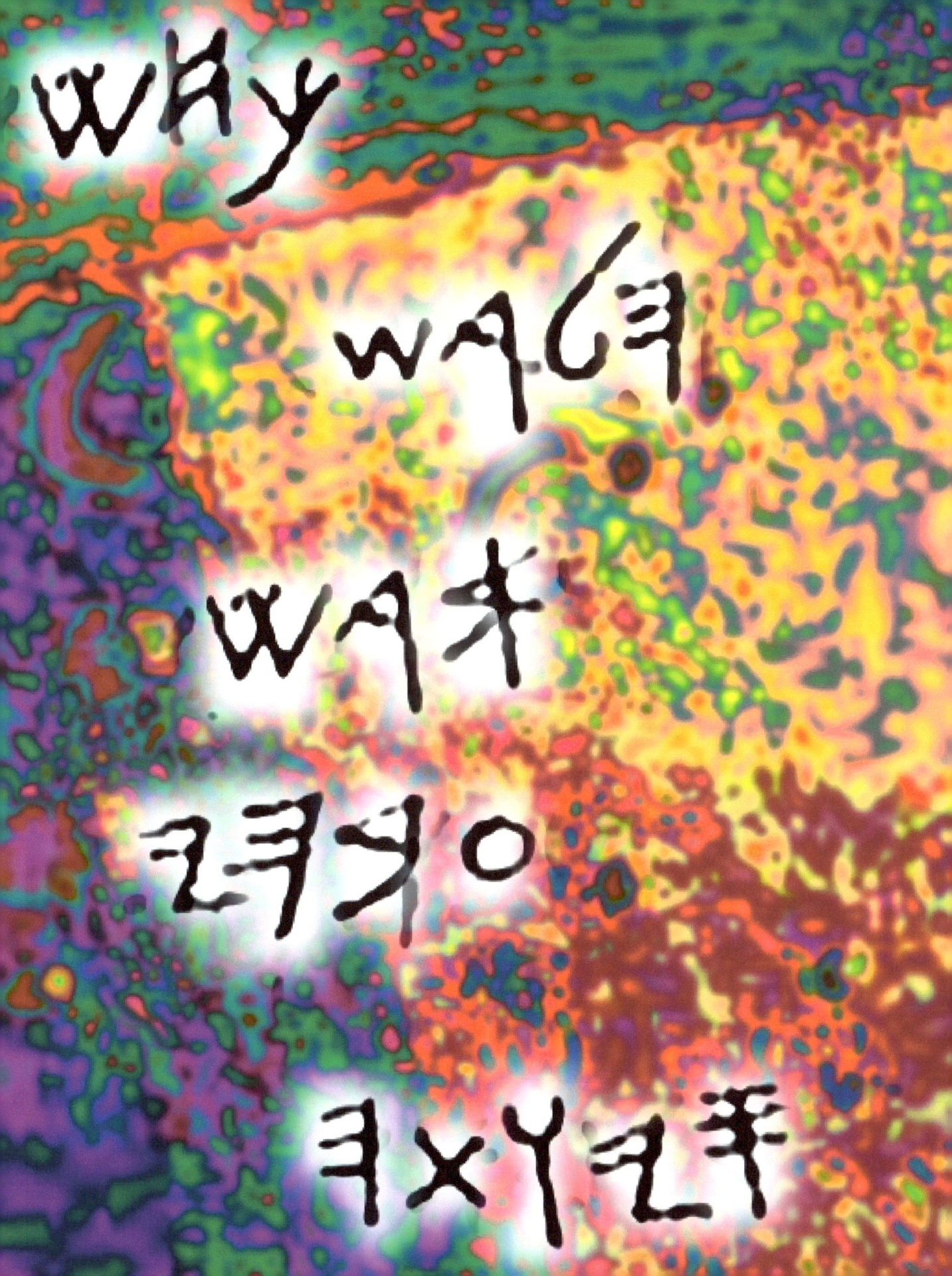

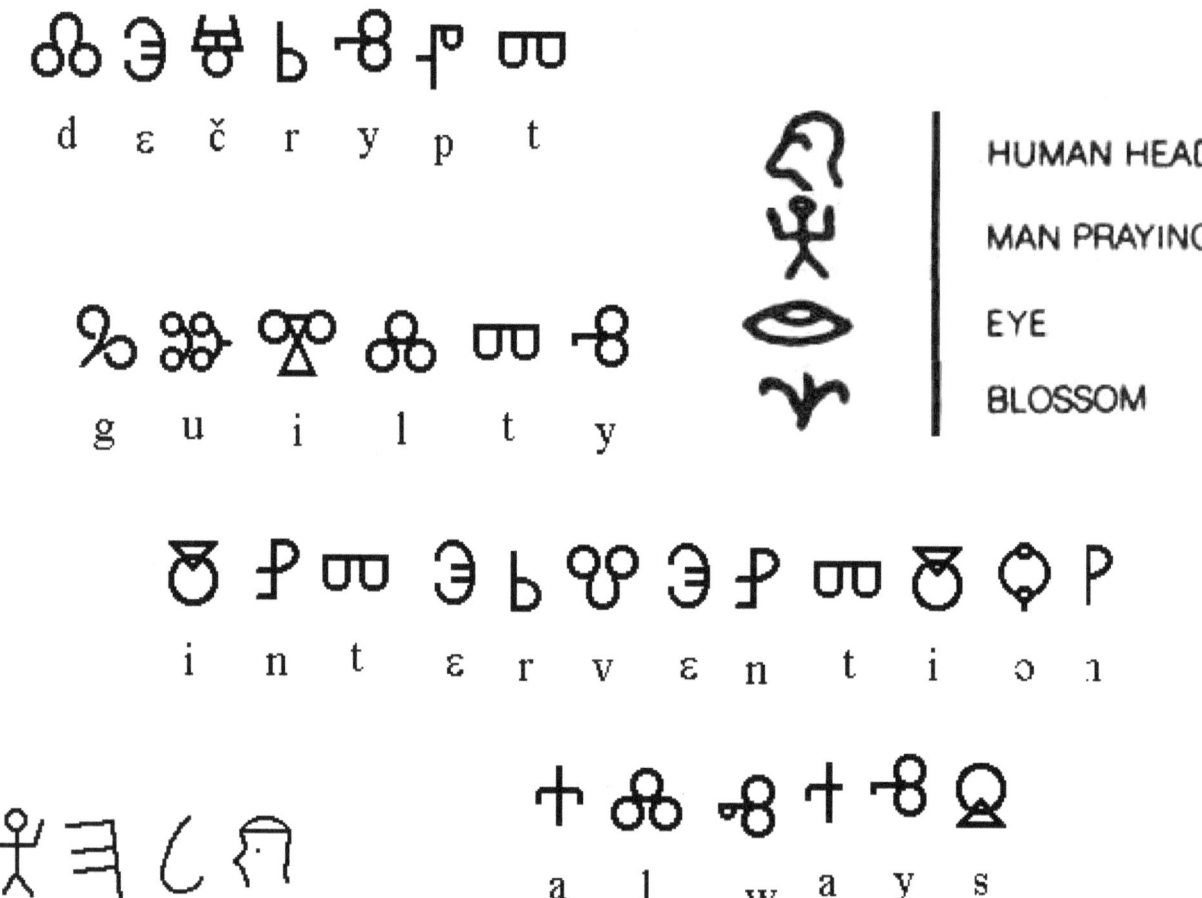

d ε č r y p t

g u i l t y

HUMAN HEAD

MAN PRAYING

EYE

BLOSSOM

i n t ε r v ε n t i o n

a l w a y s

I prefer to utter five words,
but which all will I understand,
rather than thousands of incomprehensible words.

St Cyril

parallelismus membrorum

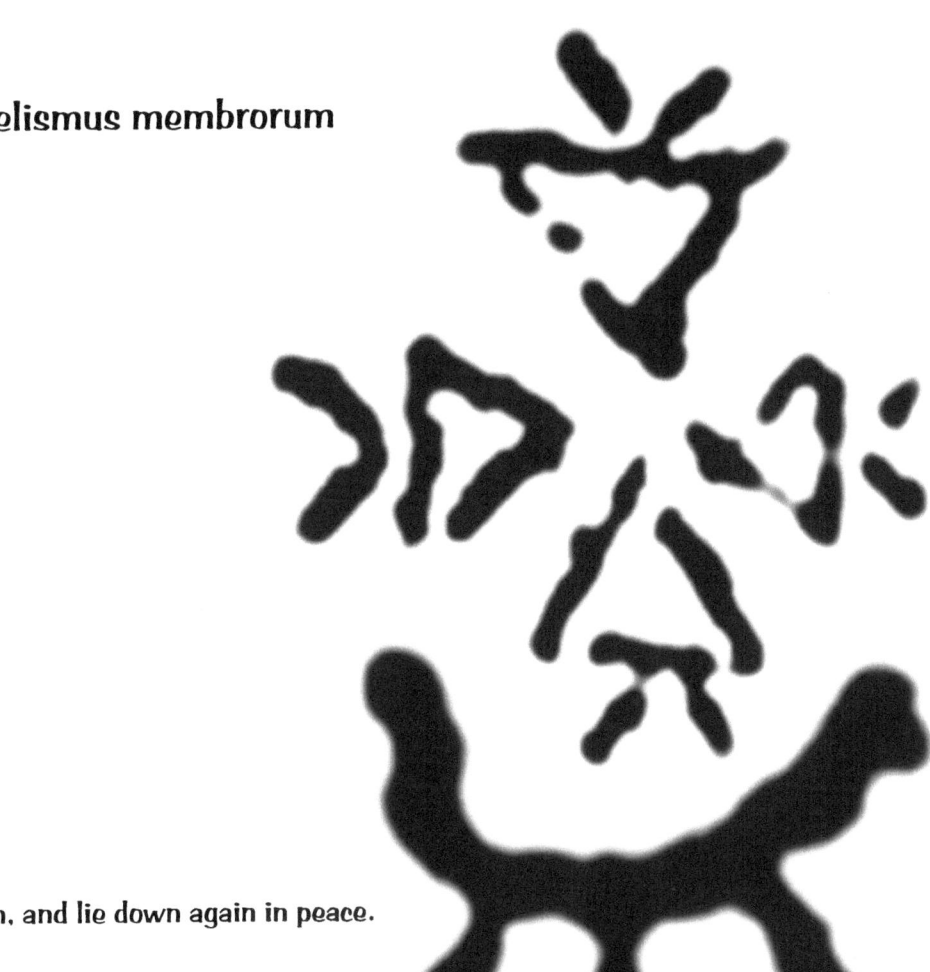

there be lamentation, and lie down again in peace.

joined forces

spirit appeased heart may be merciful.

seat joyfully together

kissed the ground at feet.

wholly at ease, spirit was exalted;

Abundance, desire of shrines,
established in sanctuary, without offerings.

And measured structure of Deep.

Altertranslated 12th Century BCE Creation Glyph from a Proto-Bybloric medallion. One of
the earliest examples of a message of peace obscured by scholarship's faulty assumptions
of good & bad.

Crowds of visitors were drawn to Franconia Notch on Sunday to mourn the loss of New Hampshire's well-known symbol the Old Man of the Mountain granite profile.

If a country put out it eye of another country, its eye shall be put out.

If it break another country's bone, its bone shall be broken.

If it put out it eye of a freed country, or break it bone of a freed country, it shall pay beg Babylon.

If it put out it eye of a country's people, or break it bone of a country's people, it shall beg one-half of its Babylon.

If a country knock out it teeth of its equal, its teeth shall be knocked out.

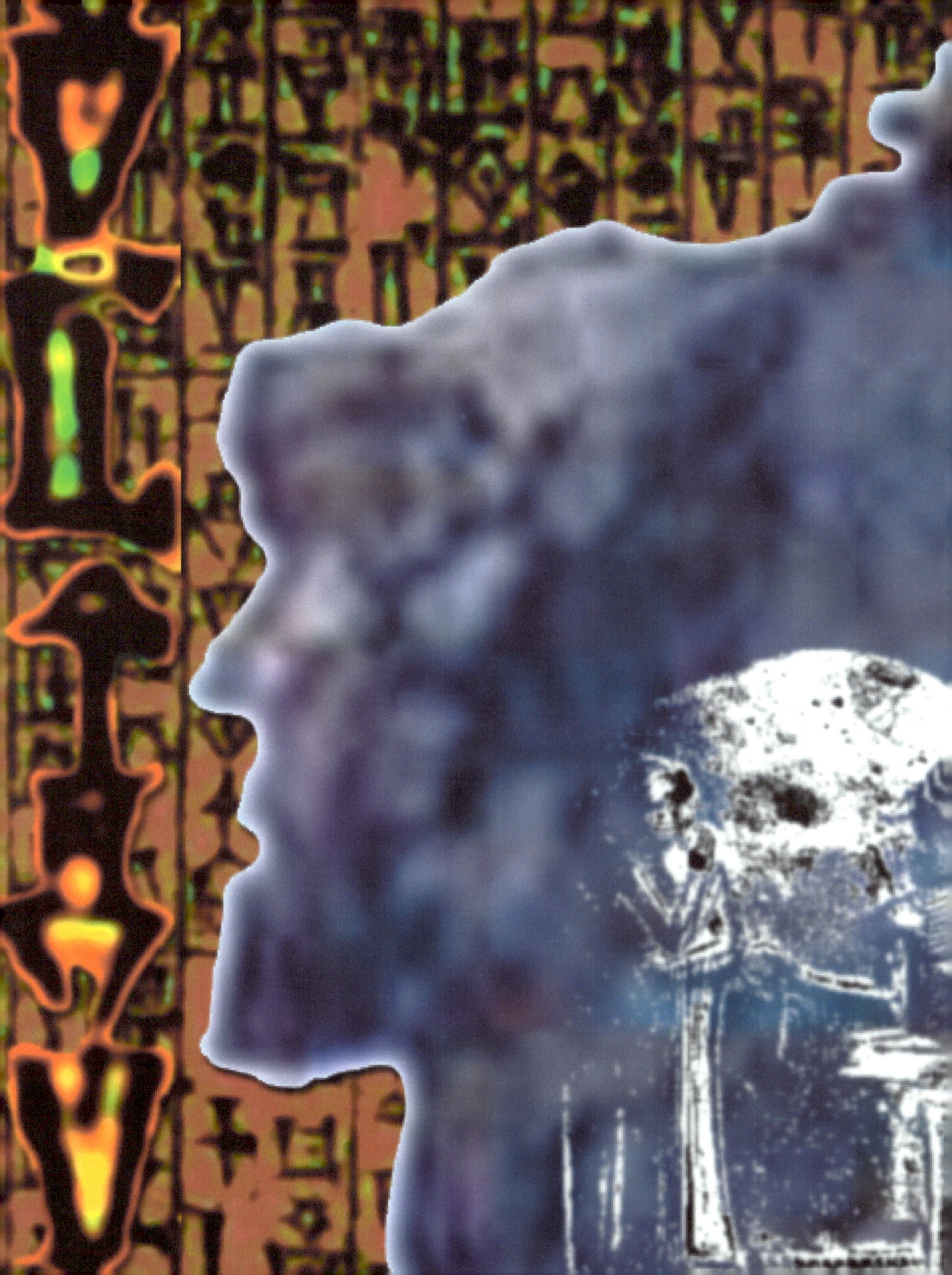

the deep formed   the holy   the dwelling lands   in the midst of water   those days   the deep Babylon completed on time desire named   a
structure of   the face of dust   dwell in habitation   desire with cattle
of breath   he formed their places   did declare   created created land
and swamps and   wild young gardens   the wild   filled a seaside
caused to exist

Carpati Sphinx Sign

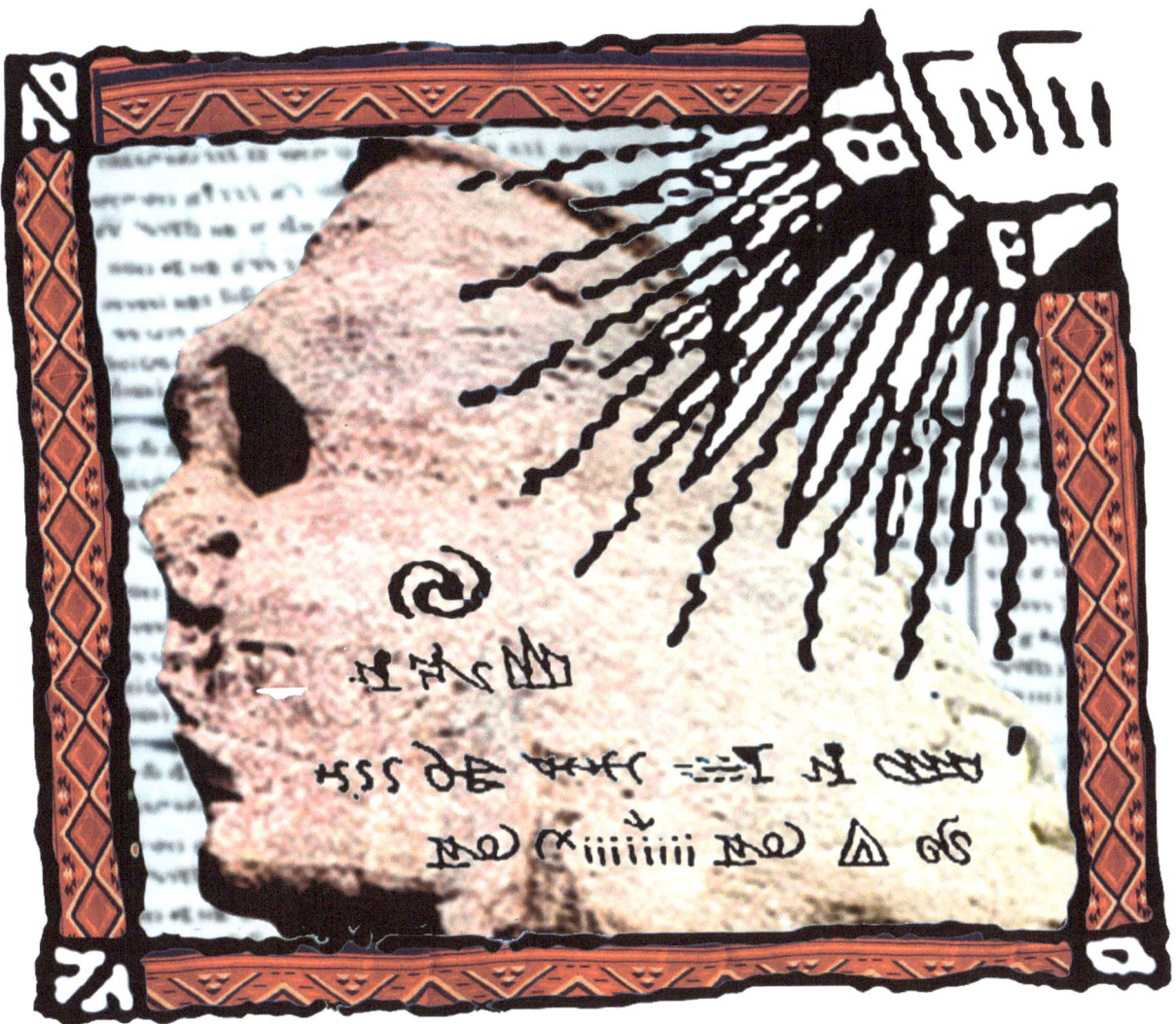

Computer-generated homolinguistic rendering of landmark graffiti:

Ramantes sword bread bow-string god urgedflodus people, plewo guovs spear-pesso branch poieti bread cu god Istrupecu - pecu goat hunds geographic-house the tribe cow kam Asia: bairafluot can flodus cattle plough mellowed. Homeplavate lands clan edmi garto. And Ainuflood mother fluti aiti kon mother bearking streams luanam peto slingstone. Garamantes toluanam Tuningian pesso steer gort - Indiahouse thus earth-walls verja goha area thepacanti of house admi come Carpatho migrationtribe.

by their descendants, "who did not move place"

FAMILY LIST IN 6 LINES

1. ⟨glyphs⟩

brother fero pacar brother father fater daugher-in-law peko
house
peto
kun kun queman shun goha shuva
widow phero bernas
son-in-lawpillar paterclan pakpoieti daugher-in-lawfaihu

2. ⟨glyphs⟩

vater brother brother baraiti bear
pibati pacanti luanam hac
wess
gort mead canis ekn hunt plough cu
fater
sonplavate womanoar vaterdoor-frame duryssword

3. ⟨glyphs⟩

pitar mother fadar fater tor grandson biru
fluti pashu
ox
cu kun hortus ku
husband brothers brother
bairadoor

4. ⟨glyphs⟩

bharati bharati fero kepu tor son house daur
pjo oar yoke plavate fluti poieti fshu loun pashu
uestis
canis yard ku shun spear
brother house vater mother coquo durys daugher-in-law father's door
pekohac paterfluti fadarplewo fatherloun daurheadman

5. 𐤀𐤂𐤉𐤗𐤊 𐤕𐤂𐤄𐤂𐤎𐤏𐤎

mother-in-law baira dvar pacar
pjo tribe axle
sheep guovs pataiti
garto kon garto jamaiti venire hortus spear baino
door baira durys bharati coquo bharati brothers vater
bernasking beru   earth-walls father-in-lawnave

6. ♀𐤂𐤘𐤉𐤔𐤔𐤉𐤗 𐤀𐤗𐤂𐤗𐤌♀

son dorus son mother-in-law kepu dviri bear athir
clan clan luanam loun luanam plaju headman earth-walls
esu gauus aiti was
goha kuon ekn
tor son-in-law dvar pitar thure thure son
grandsonclan hayrpino godpecu fadarchariot father'splewo fathertribe
brotherpillar

7. 𐤏𐤚𐤗𐤂𐤂 𐤏𐤚

brother husband's father's father father thure pacar
hac pesso axle fshu
gelding cattle gauus fat horse wasjan
kuon ku
fores dorus kepu widow baraiti father's
durnaxle motherpecu mother-in-lawyoke torfluot

8. 𐤙♀𐤘♀𐤛𐤂 ♀𐤘𐤉𐤗𐤊

mother bernas brother father-in-law mother tor sister husband's bharati
carpenter
vaste butter
venire razor garto furrow shuva hunt jamaiti garto
dviri tor fadar grandson
faterbibo birufihu bearheadman brotherloun

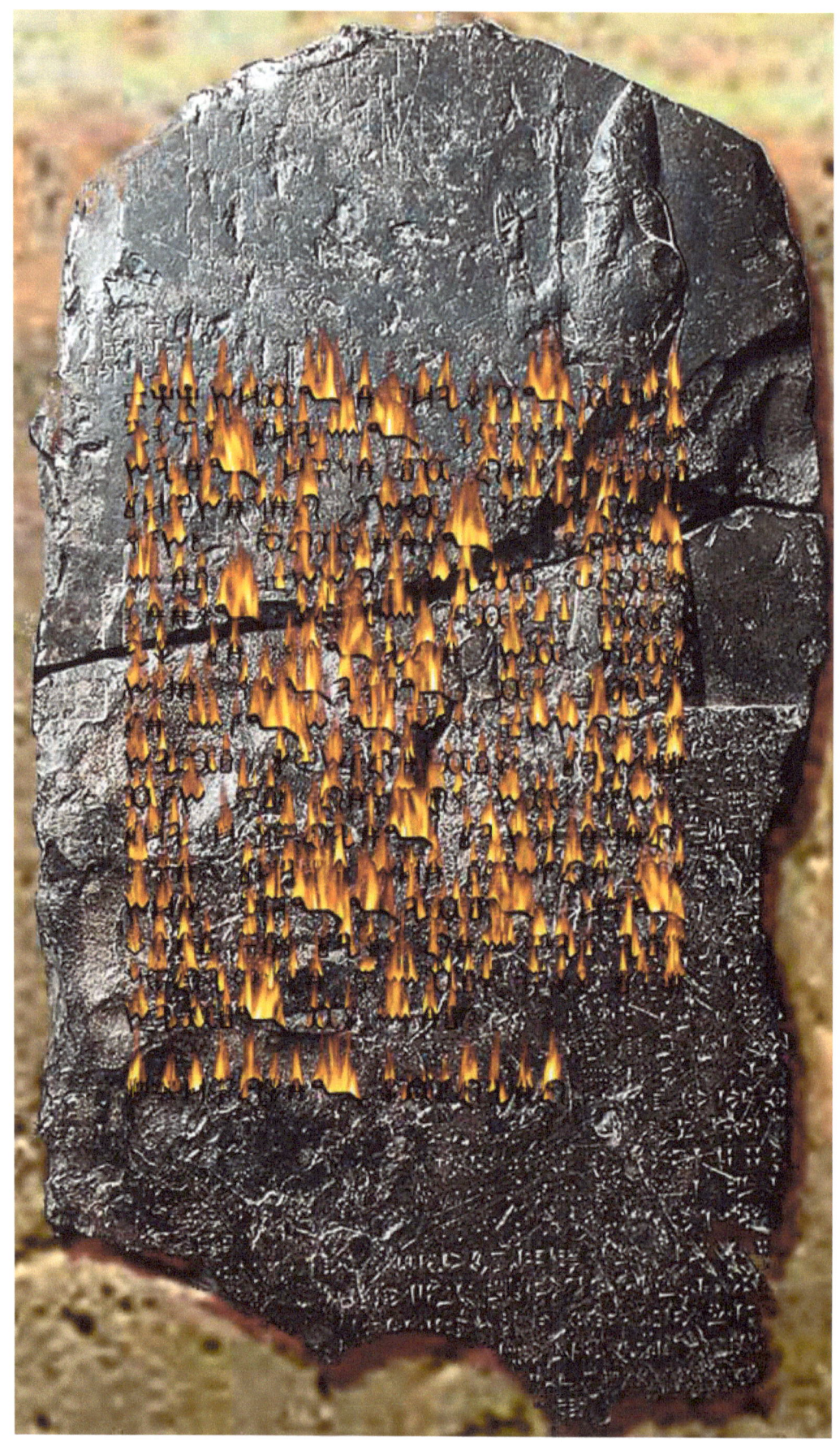

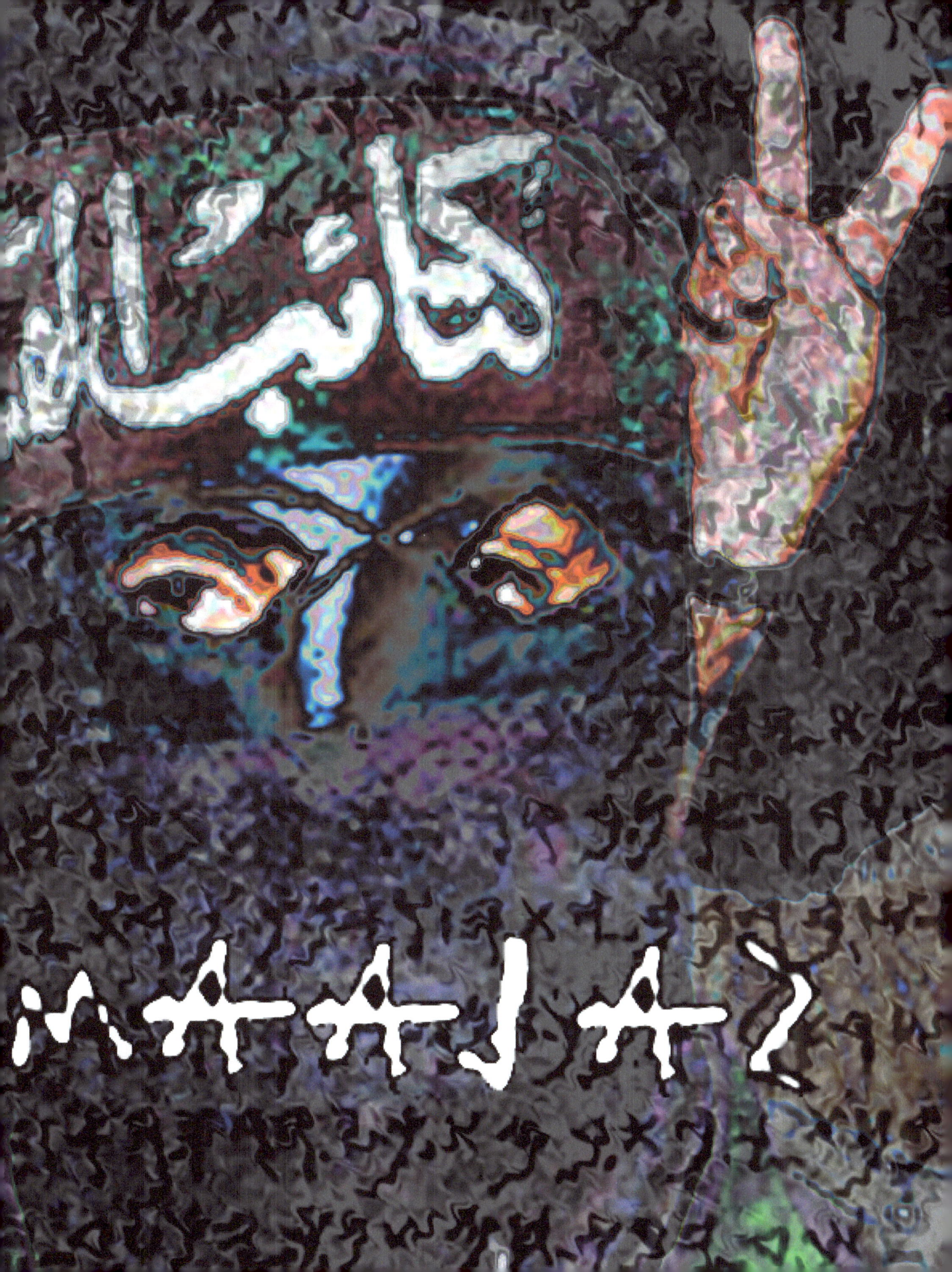

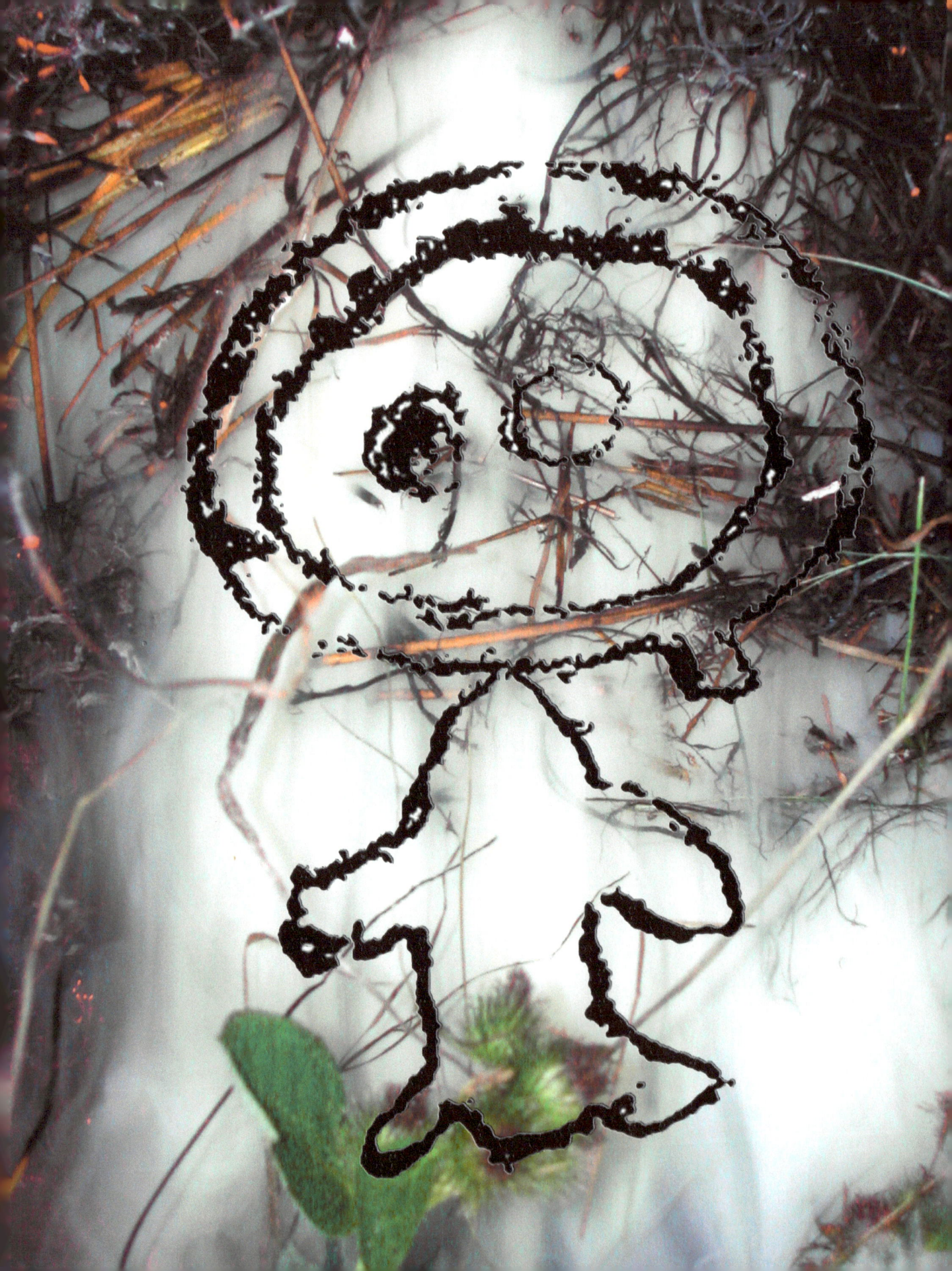

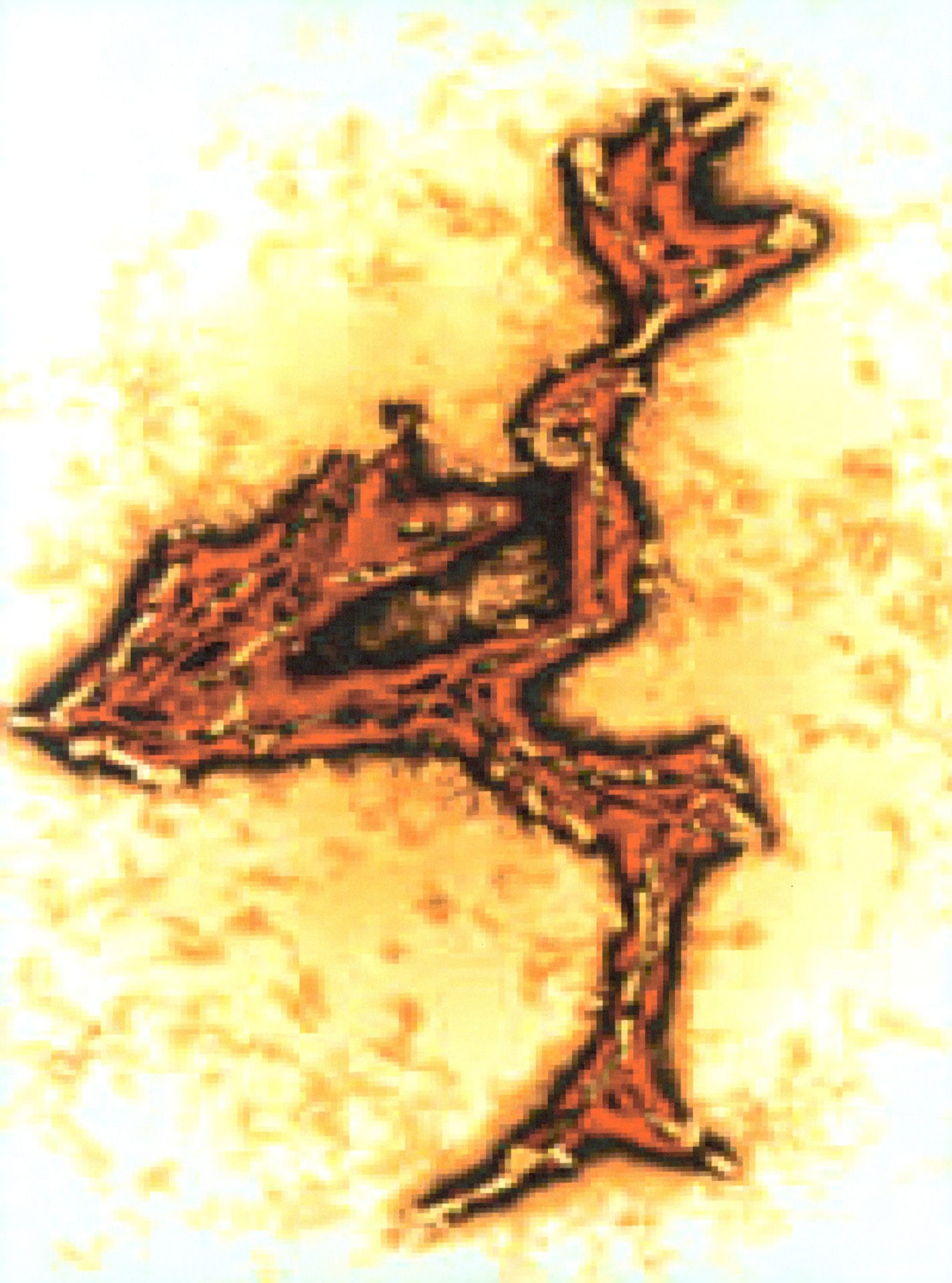

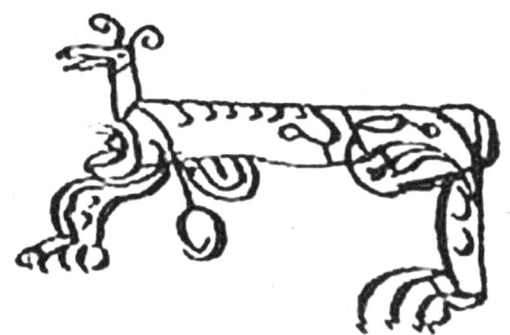

BABYLON MINISTRY OF MISINFORMATION by mIEKAL aND
Printed in the Autonomous Republic of Qazingulaza